Table of Contents

Our Friend, The Bee

Insect, Arthropod, Hymenoptera Apis mellifera, Honeybee

Do you like honey? It tastes delicious, doesn't it? Thanks to bees, you can have honey almost anytime you wish. You see, bees make honey.

I´d like to help you learn how bees get honey to your table...

So, let me tell you a story about our friend, the bee.

Bees are part of the *Arthropod* insect family. They are called *Apis mellifera* and are the **only** insect that makes food for people.

Why Are Bees So Important For You & Me?

Bees Are Good For People And The Environment

Honey is a lifesaver. If you are stuck without anything to eat, you can eat just honey. You will have all the vitamins, minerals and even water you need. It is a popular replacement for sugar because it is a pure product of nature.

When you spread a little honey on a piece of bread and eat it, your tongue gets the same sweet taste sensation it would get from big, baked donuts. Do you know which one is healthier?

There is a lot of research about how honey can help your body. Some people believe honey can help treat allergy attacks, joint pain, bug bites, tummy aches and itching.

Did you know bees are responsible for flowers as well as the plants and fruits we eat? They use their bodies and movement to help spread pollen all over the earth as they fly. This keeps our planet stocked with food.

Of course, other creatures spread pollen, too. Butterflies and hummingbirds are two good examples. But only the bee is able to make pollen into honey.

How Bees Grow

The Life Cycle Of A Bee

Our bee friends develop almost like any other insect. First, their mom, the Queen Bee, lays her eggs in a tiny cell much like a room. The cell is located in the **honeycomb**.

There is a baby bee or *larva* growing inside each egg. It takes three days for the egg to hatch. When the larva is out of the egg, it has room to grow. Over an eight-day period, the larva sheds its skin five times. The skin gives the larva the food it needs to grow bigger.

When the last skin is gone, the larva goes into the **pupa** stage. This is a quiet growing period that lasts nine days.

Finally, the color of a bee´s body changes to golden-brown or black with pale orange or yellow rings on the abdomen. As adults, they can fly away when they are three weeks old.

The bee family tree has the Queen Bee as the head of the family. All the little eggs she hatches become female worker bees or male mates.

The Bee´s Body

Anatomy Of A Bee

Bee bodies are like all insects with three main parts: **head, thorax** and **abdomen**.

Bees have a remarkable sense of distance, movement and color.

Head:

- Two *antennae* that bend to help them stay aware of their surroundings

- Two big eyes called *compound eyes*, one on each side of their head. These two eyes have thousands of tiny lenses.

- Three regular eyes on top

- One mouth, called the ***mandible***. It acts like a scooper to move food around

- One ***proboscis*** that acts like a straw to suck in nectar

- Small hairs called ***palpii*** that are like whiskers on a dog or cat. They help the bee smell and taste food flavors.

Thorax:

- The Thorax has three parts.

- Bees have six legs, like all other insects. One pair of legs is attached to each of the three parts of the thorax. The first two pairs of legs in the front have hairs for cleaning. The back pair of legs have hairs called baskets that are used for collecting pollen.

- They also have two pairs of wings. The front wings are larger and hooked to the smaller back wings that are like flaps on an airplane wing. Honeybees can flap their wings at 200 beats per second. That is why you can hear them buzz.

Abdomen:

- The abdomen has small openings so the bee can breathe.

- There is a stinger hidden at the back end of the abdomen.

- The honeybee has a specialized stomach that holds the nectar or water sucked up by the proboscis. It stays there until the honeybee returns to the hive to deposit the liquid in the nest.

Where The Bee Calls Home

The Beehive

The beehive is the outside shell of the bee´s home. You can find beehives in piles of rocks, hollow trees or in caves.

Young worker bees make the hive with beeswax from a sticky substance in their abdomen. It coats the floor of the hive. The worker bees use the same substance to build little rooms, called **honeycombs**. Each room has six sides and will hold an egg and a larva. Or it can be used to hold honey.

Most worker bees have a life span of only six weeks. They start out as workers in the hive, making honeycombs, cleaning the hive, taking in honey, and caring for the larvae.

When a worker bee is about ten days old, she develops the gland that helps to produce honey. Female workers are the bees that fly out and look for food from many types of plants and flowers. They put the nectar in their pollen pouch.

While the bee is flying home a special fluid from the gland mixes with the pollen. When they are back in the hive, they spit up the fluid onto their tongue and transfer it to another worker bee's tongue. When they do this, the liquid in the fluid evaporates and it turns into honey.

The honey is stored in the honeycomb rooms, where it can be collected for you to eat. Or the worker bees can use their glands to turn the honey into more wax to build more honeycomb rooms for the hive.

The Bee Colony

A City of Bees

There are loner bees and social bees. Other kinds of bees prefer to be alone and take care of just their little family. But honeybees are social.

That means they love to hang out with other families and share the work. They are very smart and have ways to communicate with each other.

A colony of bees is similar to a small village. The Queen Bee is the head of the colony. She controls the colony's population and activities.

The colony works all summer to collect the food they need to survive the winter. Since plants and flowers that have nectar grow in warm weather, that´s when the bees work hardest.

In the winter, they huddle up in the hive and keep each other warm, while feeding off the honey.

The Leader Of The Colony

The Queen Bee

The Queen Bee lays all the eggs in the hive, placing only one egg in each honeycomb. She makes sure that there are always enough bees to keep the hive and colony operating. During the warm months, she can lay up to 2,500 eggs per day!

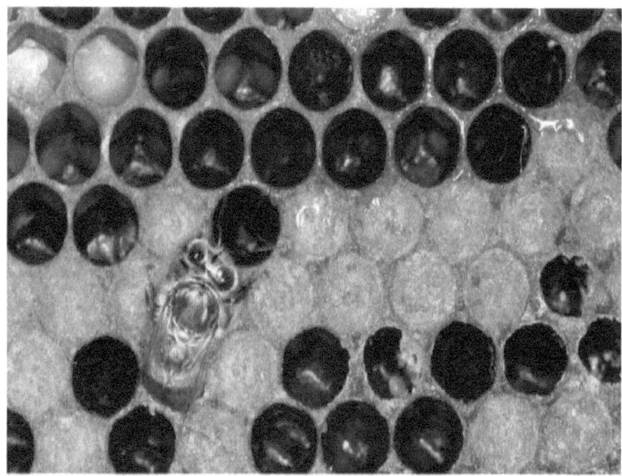

The queen can live to be five years old. If the queen dies, the female workers decide who the new queen will be. They give her extra portions of "royal jelly" (a stronger mix of honey) to make her strong so she can lay her eggs.

Male bees, called ***drones***, are around for the spring and summer months. They have to keep the queen fertilized so she can fill up the hive with eggs.

In the winter, when bees go to "sleep", the males are sent away. There are not enough supplies in the hive to support them in the winter months.

Bees: One of Man's Very Best Friends

Bee Keeping

By now, I´m sure you´re beginning to see how hard bees really work. They have to build their hives, add honeycombs, elect a queen who lays all the eggs, and send worker bees out to get nectar and pollen so they can come back home to make honey!

I get tired just thinking about it!

Over time, people have found a way to make life easier for the bees and get more honey for humans to enjoy.

Beekeepers buy or build the foundation for bees to live in. Professional beekeepers create large boxes with trays that encourage the bees to build their honeycombs.

Other beekeepers who want to raise bees in their yard build a smaller version of the hive with the same interior to attract bees.

Beekeepers buy a Queen Bee and place her in the new hive. She attracts the other bees to come and join her. Soon the colony is thriving with an entire family of honey producing bees.

As the bees make honey, the beekeepers can remove the drawers that have honey and spin it to remove the honey from the honeycombs. They return the drawers with the honeycombs back to the hive so the bees can start all over again.

Homemade Honey

The Honey Harvest

The beekeeper wants what is best for the bees as well as the honey. That´s why he takes great care when making the hives and harvesting the honey.

A nice hat with a net veil, thick gloves and smock make up the beekeeper's uniform. Beekeepers are careful not to make sudden or quick movements.

The female worker bees will use those hidden stingers if they are scared. If she senses danger, one little honeybee worker can call *all* her fellow workers into action!

One thing that can prevent the bees from warning each other is smoke. Collecting smoke from a wood fire and using bellows to blow it into the hive makes the bees think there might be a fire. When this happens, they get busy eating honey so when they are moved by the beekeeper; they are ready to occupy a new hive that has no honey.

Beekeepers also know a good harvest of honey depends on the bee´s food. Planting bee friendly flowers, living near a garden, or having a farm nearby helps the bees find food easily.

Some people say that eating honey from a beehive near where you live, will keep you healthier than honey from the store. That is why many people decide to raise bees and harvest honey of their own.

They are helping the environment, harvesting healthy food for people and enjoying a fun hobby.

The Bee Circle Of Life

What Is Pollination?

When bees visit orchards, gardens or farms and collect pollen, they scatter that pollen as they fly from plants to flowers to fruits. The growth cycle of food depends on pollen being spread as fertilizer.

With the help of butterflies and hummingbirds, the bees are an important part of our ability to eat healthy foods.

Think of all the fruits and vegetables you enjoy eating. Bees help farmers grow things like: melons, berries, nuts and greens.

Bees Like Colors, Smell & Shapes

Flowers Bees Like Best

You probably think flowers have pretty colors and smell wonderful just for you. Sorry, but flowers care more about bees, butterflies and hummingbirds. The bright colors attract bees and the fragrance promises fine nectar for them to gather.

The shape of the flower determines how much pollen the bee can collect on its fuzzy body.

The bee´s big compound eyes are able to pick out the right flower in a second and the antennae and hairy legs help smell and taste which nectar will be good.

Here are a few of the bee´s favorite flowers:

Now that you know all about bees, honey and flowers, go find some flowers you think bees would like. Look for brightly colored, sweet-smelling flowers that have lots of pollen. You are sure to find some honeybees buzzing busily nearby.

When you are done, go and treat yourself to some tasty toast with honey!

Fun Honeybee Facts

Bees are truly fascinating little creatures! Here are some surprising facts about the honeybee you might not know...

- Honeybees have been on the earth for millions of years!

- Honeybees are the only insects that produce food for people to eat.

- Honey is the only food that has all the vitamins, minerals, enzymes, and water you need to stay alive!

- The honeybee has an excellent sense of smell. It can tell hundreds of different kinds of flowers apart and knows whether they have pollen or nectar from meters away!

- The buzzing noise a honeybee makes comes from its wings beating 200 times per second. Honeybees can fly up to 15 miles per hour and as far as 6 miles.

- A honeybee can visit up to 100 flowers during one collection trip!

- Even though its brain is no bigger than a sesame seed, the honeybee has an amazing ability to learn and remember things. It can even make complex calculations about the distances it travels and the amount of pollen it collects.

- One colony of bees is made up of between 20,000 and 60,000 honeybees, plus their Queen Bee. The worker bees are all females, live roughly 6 weeks long and do all the work in the hive!

- The Queen Bee can live to be 5 years old and is the only bee that lays eggs. During summer, when it´s important for the hive to reach maximum strength, she can lay as many as 2500 eggs a day!

- The male bees, or drones, are bigger than the worker bees and don´t have stingers. They are only there for mating and don´t do any of the work in the hive.

- Only the female worker bees can sting but they die once they do. The Queen Bee has a stinger but she never leaves the hive and so, never uses it.

- Bees communicate with each other by dancing on the honeycomb. Depending on the exact movements they use, they can tell their sister honeybees about types of food they have discovered and where it is located.

It´s a "Bee Poem"!

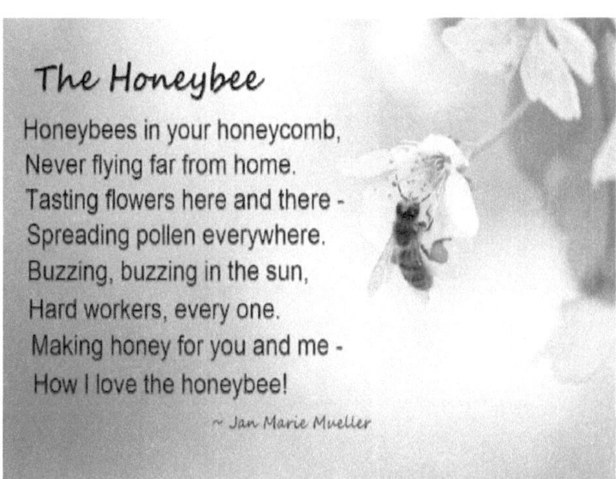